Inversion and the Perspective-Based Safety Culture

Brian O. Owens

HIGH LONESOME PUBLISHING

High Lonesome Publishing
2018

Inversion and the Perspective-Based Safety Culture.

ISBN: 978-0-578-43680-7

Contact:
High Lonesome Publishing.
bowens@hl-publishing.com

CONTENTS

INVERSION

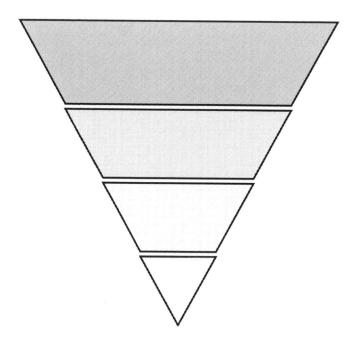

"A situation in which something is changed so that it is the opposite of what it was before."

—*Cambridge Dictionary*

Introduction:

Learning from Storytelling

WHEN I WAS YOUNG, I was enamored with my grandfathers. They were both amazing storytellers, and they offered little resistance when I asked them to recount their experiences from bygone decades. I focused intently when I could see I was in for another tale, whether sitting around a campfire, resting on a front porch, or gathered in a family living room. They used storytelling to help me learn important lessons.

I struggled with fractions as a kid. My mom's dad, a farmer for most of his life, took me aside and said, "Your mama tells me you're having trouble with fractions in school."

I reluctantly nodded yes.

He walked me over to the rows of corn in his garden. "How many rows of corn do you see in this patch?"

I counted them and told him.

"Good. Now, how many of those rows are

watered?"

Again, I gave him my answer.

He said, "It looks like you can do fractions just fine."

And just like that, I got it: a fraction was a part of a whole. It only took something simple to make the lightbulb go on.

I can remember wanting to be a truck driver like my dad's dad. I was fascinated with the big rigs and thought if he could do it, then so could I. Dad told me there was more to it than just driving, and if I was going to drive like Grandad did, then I'd need to do it safely. He said Grandad had achieved a remarkable safety milestone in his career. When I asked what it was, he told me to go ask him myself.

Grandad's remarkable milestone turned out to be a closet full of safety awards for four million miles of accident/violation-free driving, something I still struggle to wrap my head around, especially considering the compliance measures for his vocation. When I asked how he did it, he chuckled and said, "One mile at a time." I still marvel at the power in that answer's simplicity.

What struck me most about these wise men was that I later found out that neither one of them had a formal education beyond eighth grade. How was it that these men who probably wouldn't have been able to pass the battery of tests I took to graduate high school could be so intelligent, wise, and insightful? How could their lessons be so powerful and remain such a focal point in my life, even to this day? They weren't certified. They had no credentials or accolades to support a position worthy of bestowing knowledge upon other people. Nonetheless, they were teachers, educators who gave effective and applicable knowledge to those fortunate enough to listen.

Through my grandfathers, I learned a valuable lesson, one I'm not even sure they knew they were teaching: one of the most powerful tools a person can use is perspective.

My grandfathers mastered the art of teaching through storytelling, and I saw it in other places, too. I noticed it in school. I took notes until my hand cramped, filling an entire notebook with items to study in preparation for an exam, complete with circling, underlining, and highlighting. That did little to actually ensure I understood the subject matter. It only served to help me pass the test, and even then, sometimes only barely. But, if a teacher incorporated a story into the lesson or made a relatable connection to something I knew, I understood that portion of the material and retained the information.

I also noticed it in church. I was a disheveled and distracted kid in the pew, paying no attention and doodling cartoons on the bulletin—that is, until the preacher launched into a story. Then I dropped the pencil, perked up, and listened to everything he said. As soon as he deviated from the mundane drone of scripture, it was like a switch flipped in my brain that made me want to pay attention. As many hours as I invested in sermon lectures growing up, the lessons I remember the most were ones from stories.

The human psyche is attracted to relatable analogy. From the time we are young, we love lessons taught in the form of stories. Nursery rhymes and children's tales demonstrate the morals of their stories. Philosophy draws from the same well. Songwriters, poets, novelists, and filmmakers also tap into this rich resource.

There's a reason storytelling is all around us: humans have the unique ability to believe in ideas. Look at religion, politics, even sports fandom. People can invest their entire being into thoughts and beliefs, creating an unyielding devotion that has the power to start wars. (Just ask "Star Wars or Star Trek" and stand back.) Ideas are the birthplace of action.

You might be wondering by now what this has to do with occupational safety and culture development. The short answer is: everything.

PART I

INVERSION:
RECOGNIZING THE NEED
FOR CHANGE

1

The Behavioral Formula and the Foundation of Culture

I ONCE ATTENDED a company health and safety meeting after a rash of incidents, and a high-ranking executive wanted answers. The Safety Pyramid was used to as a prop to help convey his frustration. I was quite familiar with the pyramid, having used it in my teachings early in my career as a health and safety professional.

The Safety Pyramid was based on work performed by a safety engineer named H. W. Heinrich, author of the 1931 book *Industrial Accident Prevention: A Scientific Approach*. Mr. Heinrich deduced that one industrial fatality sat atop a collective compilation of unsafe behaviors and increasingly severe injuries.

The concept took on the shape of a pyramid, with the fatal incident at the top, and the broad base of unsafe behaviors at the bottom. The idea behind the pyramid suggested that the better you control the risky behaviors at the bottom, the better chance you have of eventually eliminating the fatality at the top.

Basic premise of the traditional Safety Pyramid.

Back to the meeting. A senior safety official suggested the organization should focus on the upper half of the pyramid, where the really bad stuff happens. He theorized that emphasizing that part of the pyramid would work as a scare tactic to make employees stay safe.

I left that meeting with a thought I couldn't shake. It kept me up late into the night. I asked myself, "How is that good enough?" All of it, even the pyramid as a whole. How was the entire concept good enough? How was starting so late in the game acceptable to those of us charged with ensuring and facilitating a sustainable safety culture?

It bothered me. I felt like we were completely missing the point. In a state of exhaustion, I drew the outline of a pyramid. As I fumbled with the paper, I accidentally brushed the corner and flipped it upside down. The pyramid was inverted. My feeling turned into an idea. I thought, "Maybe it's *not* good enough."

Historically, much of occupational safety and health was built on a foundation of compliance and enforcement. Don't believe me? Look up a computer game produced in the early 1980s called *Hard Hat Mack* and see what the game developers thought about OSHA. (Hint: OSHA is the villain in the game.)

Despite its roots, there is an exciting movement in occupational safety and health that has been taking shape over the last decade or so. Many companies have started understanding the power of the behavioral aspect of workplace safety. These programs, sometimes called Behavior-Based Safety (BBS), have started pursuing avenues that nurture employee behavioral buy-in and promoting attempts at building organizational cultures.

While I am a proponent of behavior-focused programs, and I believe that the pathway to a culture built around the pursuit of zero incidents goes through behavior, I don't believe it starts there. My experience and research tell me it starts much earlier.

Safety doesn't exist all by itself, like a thing in a vacuum. You can't replenish your safety levels like engine oil, nor can you go to the store and buy another box of safety. Safety is the byproduct of ideological buy-in and the resulting behavior, and can therefore not materialize on its own. That said, what makes people believe and behave the way they do, creating or inhibiting safety along the way?

The *Merriam-Webster Dictionary* defines culture as "the set of shared attitudes, values, goals, and practices that characterizes an institution or organization." Culture is then, by definition, uniform behavior among people with common objectives by which a collective identity is created. Behavior, it seems, has a direct effect on culture. If that's the case, can we assume that behavior is a pre-fabricated product we can simply insert into the business model, instantly creating a culture customized to our liking? If it were that easy, you probably wouldn't be reading this.

The *Business Dictionary* defines behavior as "a response of an individual or group to an action, environment, person, or stimulus." If behavior is an effect in response to a cause, then how can a company build and sustain a safety culture, even one grounded in behavior, without first considering what environmental factors and stimuli created its employees' behavior in the first place?

Imagine casting individual links of chain at different places around the world before flying them all to a central location to be linked together and made into one chain. Once the links are assembled, how would you definitively confirm the continuity and strength of the chain without testing it first? You couldn't, because you have no way of knowing if each link was made as robust as the next. You don't know if all the links contain the correct materials at acceptable proportions to withstand a strain. You are essentially left with three choices:

A) Take the chain at face value and hope it holds up.

B) Rely on a strength test or x-ray as part of a quality assurance procedure to make sure the chain will hold up under stress.

C) Not use the chain.

Let's now compare this chain to your workforce. Does it not consist of people from different locations, different walks of life, different backgrounds, different exposures and influences? Some may have been exposed to healthy methodology, proper training, and correct safety culture development, thus making them a solid link in the chain of workplace culture. Others... not so much. It is only after they join the team and are put under a workload that their weaknesses become exposed in the form of unsafe behavior, which likely existed before they even joined your workforce.

Since using hope as a tactic is not ideal for cultural development, it would appear that the answer to this dilemma requires a proactive means to ensure the strength of the employee chain before putting it to work. But what does that look like?

The answer involves breaking down behavioral development from the point of view of the individual. What series of circumstances—and in what order—eventually creates a person's behavior and their contribution to the safety culture? These events follow a progressive formula.

I call it The Behavioral Formula.

THE BEHAVIORAL FORMULA

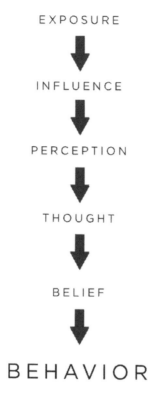

EXPOSURE

INFLUENCE

PERCEPTION

THOUGHT

BELIEF

BEHAVIOR

Our **exposures** create what we become **influenced** by, which creates the **perception** of what we think is true. Those **thoughts** turn into **beliefs**, which eventually express themselves as **behavior**. The Behavioral Formula exists in every employee.

With that in mind, consider the cultural piece. When we view the Behavioral Formula as a collective model to demonstrate cultural development in an organization, it looks like this:

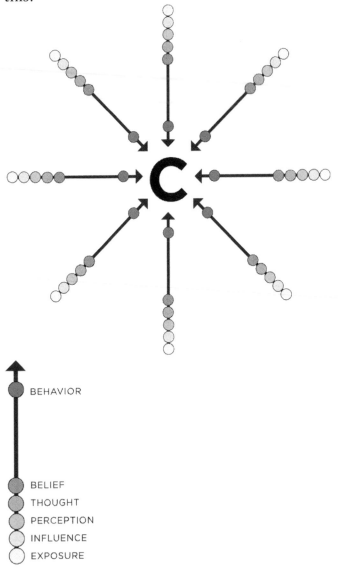

This model shows how each individual's Behavioral Formula contributes to the creation of the culture, the big C in the center. Employees' collective behavior culminates in the organization's culture.

Something many business professionals forget is that their employees are first, foremost, and always **people**. Every day, before they set foot in the door to apply for a job and long after they walk out the same door for the last time, employees are first people. It's really why they become employees in the first place. They seek employment to sustain their personal livelihoods. Employment helps people be who they want and choose to be. But how often do employers acknowledge employees' humanity? Isn't that where cultural development truly begins?

Most organizations interested in developing a behavior-based safety program jump in midstream, starting with and focusing on behavior. On the surface, that might seem logical. But that approach assumes the company is starting with a blank slate and can install whatever employee frame of mind suits the company's purposes. This approach also assumes human behavior can be controlled to produce a desired result.

Here's the problem. People aren't blank slates, and you can't control human behavior. As beings with free will, people make decisions that result in consequences, both good and bad.

Human behavior will always be uncontrollable, regardless of how we try to restrict it.

The Behavioral Formula can be extremely effective at creating a solid link of chain. It's why people believe and behave the way they do. But existing employee behaviors, even ones that are culture-inhibitive, are the result of years of time and influences, and most companies lack the time, budget, or patience to rebuild each employee into the ideal link of chain.

What if you could plug a single element into that formula that would give you the ability to know exactly what those links of chain are made of, and as a result, know that the chain will hold, regardless of the workload you suspend from it?

What if I said you already possess the ability to use that element? Allow me to introduce you to the power of perspective.

2

Culture: Excellence or Compliance?

IN THE WEEKS AND MONTHS that followed my late-night revelation after the Safety Pyramid discussion, I began to piece together a better way to build a workplace safety culture. I didn't want to reinvent the pyramid so much as concentrate on a more proactive way to focus on and eliminate risk potential.

Looking at the pyramid as a sequence, it struck me as being partial, the ideology inadequate. It looked more like half of a formula that ended up being adopted as the whole concept. My major contentions with the pyramid as a sole representation of safety management were these:

1. Starting at the very bottom, the foundation, you have at-risk behavior. As I mentioned earlier, the idea here is to reduce the amount of risky behaviors

through control. But what happens when you have a single, unsafe behavior with high-energy sources such as electricity, explosives, demolition, heavy equipment operation, or driving? Obviously, one solitary, unsafe behavior can kill people instantly, taking us on a straight-line bypass to the top of the pyramid. It doesn't take a liberal smattering of close calls to end with an employee fatality. Here it can be one and done. Traditional pyramid thinking doesn't work in cases like these.

2. The pyramid is based entirely on lagging indicators, reactivity, and after-the-fact action. You can't address at-risk behavior until it occurs, and can only then take action if you see the behavior. How many at-risk behaviors are occurring that you don't even see? How do you create corrective actions without having the behavior/situation/incident to build on in the first place? Every step in the Safety Pyramid is just a lagging indicator built on the previous one.

3. You can't control human behavior. Suggesting you can, and using that as a foundational premise, weakens the rest of the concept.

Again, I had a hard time swallowing that the

Safety Pyramid as a singular concept was a good enough method to steer a company's safety incident number towards zero.

I have been a part of good groups and not so good groups. I don't mean good and bad as in morally and ethically good or bad; I just mean some worked and gelled, and some didn't. Some of these groups were employment-based, others were extracurricular, but a common thread could be found in both: the culture determined success or failure. I decided to look deeper into the "why".

What made the good cultures click, and what made the bad ones flop? I was chasing this query when I got the opportunity to go to a workplace health and safety conference that helped solidify what I was beginning to piece together in my research.

The keynote speaker said he had once been a self-managed/self-employed health and safety consultant. After the Great Recession, he was looking for creative ways to drum up new business, and a thought crossed his mind. In his office, he had filing cabinets full of the initial safety incident data collected from many companies he consulted for in the past. Perhaps if he circled back around now, several years later, and took another snapshot of the trends, he could do a comparative analysis and graph the resulting improvements. Then he could publish the scrubbed data that showed what his services were capable of rendering.

It seemed like a great idea that could produce a favorable and potentially more profitable outcome, so he pursued it. But after looking at the current safety conditions at his former clients' operations, he was disappointed to find that the trends showed only moderate improvement in some cases, if any at all. Confused, he walked away not sure how to proceed.

"If safety isn't the answer," he pondered, "because that's what I gave them, and it didn't work, then what is?" Intrigued, he went in another direction to find the answer. He examined data from some of the most successful companies at that time, including workplace safety performance. When he compared these companies side-by-side, he realized something startling: none of these companies put safety first! What they put first were the foundational ingredients: quality and excellence.

The concept of raising the bar and creating a culture of quality and excellence on purpose, as opposed to by happenstance, appealed to me. You could just as easily call it craftsmanship, follow through, best effort every time, or polish and shine. (The Japanese 5S model is a great example of this.)

Imagine an employee using a hose in the workplace as part of his normal job. He looks at his watch and realizes it is break time. Briefly taking time to turn off the hose, he drops it in on the floor and walks off. A few minutes later, another employee who doesn't see the hose walks through the area. The second employee trips on the hose, falls, and breaks his wrist, becoming a lost-time injury and being out of work for a couple of weeks.

Is this what we would call a workplace "safety issue"? The way many of us currently look at workplace safety, it may appear so. But while it became one, after the fact, I ask you first to consider what it was to begin with. It was initially a workplace quality and excellence issue in the form of poor housekeeping.

Let's say the supervisor of that area had set expectations that were grounded in quality and excellence: when you're done with the hose, roll it up; aisleways are to be kept neat and orderly; oily rags go in the oily rags bin where they belong; upset conditions require immediate notification to leadership; the final product is a true representation of the passion, craftsmanship, and effort that went into creating it.

With this shift in culture, how many "safety issues" go away in the process?

Picture the operations of a business as a dartboard, with the outer edge of the target representing compliance. Most companies plan tasks by saying, "Get the job done, and do it legally." This would be like saying, "Hit the dartboard somewhere; anywhere will do."

If that is your business plan, then what did you plan for the bad days when your aim is off, and you miss the dartboard altogether, hitting the wall instead? Without a clear target other than compliance, "good enough" becomes acceptable. That leaves you zero wiggle room when things don't go according to plan. But by creating a culture of excellence and quality, you redirect your focus to performing and delivering nothing but the best, every single time.

BULLSEYE

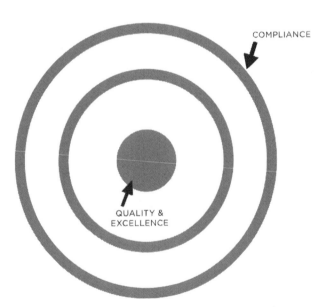

Where does your operation currently focus attention?

In other words, the bullseye on the dartboard *is* the target. Every. Single. Time. There is no other target. There is no other acceptable outcome. The excess room around your target is of little concern, because you are always expressly focused on the bullseye. When this expectation is firmly established and clearly communicated, everyone in the company lives it as part of the business culture.

In the military, there are Special Forces teams whose group titles instantly command respect. Rangers. SEALs. Delta. Why is it that these entities are synonymous with being elite? What sets them apart from other military detachments, since they all have the same high-level objective and are part of the same big picture? Similar to our dartboard analogy, these groups operate at an extremely high level of quality and excellence, accepting absolutely nothing but the best. The reputation that now precedes them is the effect of cultural maturation.

By changing the way you view your target, you systematically change the expectations. By performing under this improved point of view, you create your contingency for those bad days where you slip and miss your target: you will at least hit the board and remain in compliance!

The first step is to change the way you think. Where is your "Outrage Meter" currently calibrated to go off? In other words, when are you getting mad and slapping the table, saying, "That's enough"? If you're like most companies, that alarm goes off when too many people get hurt, property gets damaged, or both—especially if there have been several examples of this in a short time. If that's the case, why you are waiting so long to become concerned and get involved? Shouldn't your Outrage Meter be dialed all the way back to where the floor isn't swept, the truck is left messy, and the hose isn't rolled up?

By shifting the mindset, you create a better, more proactive culture.

While this might make sense in theory, you might still be wondering how to get a program like this off the ground without sending the workforce into culture shock. The best people to champion this campaign are the very people who should already possess the ability to effectively convey perspective: the leaders in the organization.

3

Culture: Perspective through Leadership

WHILE SERVING IN THE ARMY, I did a two-year stint as the Humvee driver for my Company's First Sergeant. Over time, it became apparent that he was grooming me for a transition into being a military leader. His preferred method was one he claimed had been used on him by one of his early mentors. He said that you develop your own style of leadership by looking at both the good and poor leaders you have had in the past. He said, "Ask yourself why you respected a certain leader. What about them made you willing to follow them into battle? What traits, mannerisms, qualities, and values were present in the person that command your respect?" He suggested embracing those things as a guideline for my own development.

He also suggested I recall the poor leaders I had been exposed to. "In your opinion, why were they a failure at being a leader? Why did you not respect them? What about them made you question their orders or authority?" He suggested not only shunning those characteristics, but to always remember how they made me and others feel and react. By applying these combined findings to my own development, I would arrive at a better place to embrace leadership growth than if I had drifted aimlessly.

My First Sergeant's influence helped me further recognize the value of lessons learned using the power of perspective. The man had stories aplenty and, like my grandfathers, used them to make points relevant to the circumstances, helping me see them clearly. He certainly established himself as a person I would follow into battle.

There is a big difference between leading and supervising. It is here that I feel we lose our focus, and with it, a crucial step in our cultural development. People in a leadership position have an important role in cultural development, and it goes far beyond being in a position of authority. Many people in authoritative roles see themselves as the executors of policy and procedure, and they use the power vested in them as a supervisor to enforce compliance with the policies and procedures.

While that is part of the responsibility bestowed upon leaders, what methodology they employ and how it is received by those they lead will ultimately determine success. In other words, your effort to lead is only half the handshake. Rules, regulations, and enforcement do little to ensure employee buy-in.

If using enforcement is not the most persuasive and effective way a leader can steer a culture towards being best in class, what is?

People who have made a career out of being a motivator, spokesperson, or some other position of influence all share a common quality: passion. They are driven by something that is bigger than they are as an individual, and they are loyal to their message, whatever it is. Most people who are passionate about something have been affected by an event, whether tragic or inspiring, which has played a major role in driving the passion they communicate. That event informs their perspective. They experienced a change due to sudden circumstances that led them to think, believe, and behave differently from that point on. This event directly shaped their contribution to the cultural ideology, regardless of what their earlier exposures, influences, and perceptions were.

We all know people like this, and we are familiar with the event-based perspective that created the trajectory shift in their lives. It's easy to see the power that perspective has had on them, and the way they use it to convey their message effectively.

Now suppose we could use the benefits of

perspective without waiting for an outside event to create it for us. What if we could manipulate perspective's powerful properties and use the effects to purposefully initiate a culture shift? If tragedy-based perspective has the power to change people's lives, to cause them to believe and behave differently, why can't it be used proactively, before tragedy is even born, to create a similar shift in the Behavioral Formula?

In the hands of the right people in the right leadership roles, perspective can be plugged into an employee's Behavioral Formula between Perception and Thought. This has the potential to create a behavioral change within the employee, and ultimately their cultural buy-in.

It doesn't matter what you've been exposed to. It doesn't matter what you've been influenced by. It doesn't matter what you perceive to be true. Properly placed perspective *will* change the way you think, believe, and behave from that point forward.

THE BEHAVIORAL FORMULA

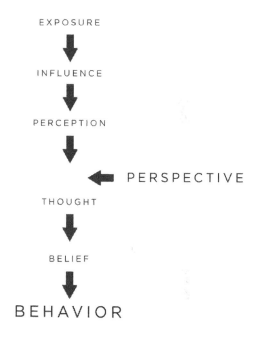

EXPOSURE

INFLUENCE

PERCEPTION

PERSPECTIVE

THOUGHT

BELIEF

BEHAVIOR

How astute are we being when placing people into leadership roles? Far too often, people are promoted into supervisory roles for no other reason than they are the most senior employees available, and therefore the most knowledgeable about the job. While this might be an attractive quality, what qualifies them to lead people?

If that question stumped you, consider these:

- How effective of a commutator is this person?
- Can they speak to all ages, genders, and

personalities simultaneously, as well as individually?
- Are they passionate?
- Do they believe in what they are saying? Do *you* believe what they are saying? (Why or why not?)
- Are they convincing? (Why or why not?)
- Do they coach and mentor, or blame and persecute?
- Do they see behavioral and cultural obstacles as problems or opportunities?

While these are not the only questions to consider when placing someone in a leadership role, they ought to be in the mix. If you are thinking in horror about who you currently have in those roles, you might have neglected these questions.

What is your company's method of leadership development and progress assurance for the incumbents? If there isn't anything formal in place, perhaps there should be. These are, after all, people the company has chosen to trust with the responsibility of safekeeping the formal health and safety program, compliance with policies and procedures, and developing the culture which helps ensure the protection of the employees.

It's one thing to have your eyes on the result, safely shrouded in the best intentions. But if you fail to consider the individual components of your action plan, don't be surprised when the result is different than what you intended.

Are you building supervisors or leaders? Are they truly representing the company's cultural ideology? Is perspective part of your plan to achieve the results you want? If not, can you rationally be frustrated when things aren't working out the way you'd like them to?

4

Controls, Risk Tolerance, and the Path to Zero

Picture a typical safety training class for new hires, complete with the usual death-by-PowerPoint flair and check-the-box compliance-based presentations. When it is time to review the company's program that protects against falls, the class is informed that the company has taken aggressive steps to ensure the safety of those who access the roof. These steps include having painted a red line on the roofs of every building on the property to delineate where OSHA requires workers to wear fall protection, and establishing a "zero tolerance rule" to forbid putting one toe over that line without fall protection. Going the extra mile to ensure the employees understand how important safety is, the company has posted signs on the roof, every 15 feet along the red line, as reminders of the OSHA standard and the company's zero tolerance policy.

To the untrained eye, this may appear to be a solid effort, a great use of controls to avoid potential risk. Hold that thought.

Let's take pause to look at the Hierarchy of Controls. "Controls" is an industry safety word meaning whatever is in place to make a situation safer for the worker. The hierarchy lists controls in descending order, from most to least effective:

- Elimination.
- Substitution.
- Engineering.
- Administration.
- Personal Protective Equipment (PPE).

Elimination means removing the hazard altogether. It is the unicorn of the safety world. We'd love to be in the presence of it. We've even heard a few tales of it happening in other places, maybe from a friend of a friend, but we have never seen it for ourselves. This is why it is firmly planted at the top and, although elusive, should be pursued actively, because it is 100% effective.

Substitution is a swap that reduces or eliminates the hazard. Some folks in the safety world don't even recognize this as a control, but I've included it because I've made good use of it in the past. I once worked for a company that did pipeline coating. One of our clients wanted us to use a certain product that was very flammable and was listed as a potential carcinogen. I called them back and said, "Look, this is nasty stuff. We have another client, very similar to you, that uses this other coating product instead. They love it. It's a lot safer for our folks to apply. Would it be okay with you if we used this instead?" Not only were they grateful that we came to them with the suggestion, but they were fine with the safer alternative. We reduced the risk to our employees with an effective substitution control.

Engineering is where you build, make, or fabricate a way to reduce or eliminate the hazard. Engineering controls are usually effective, but they sometimes come with a big price tag since they can involve technical or mechanical applications created by folks with a lot of letters after their names on their business cards. Even so, engineering controls remain one of the most effective methods of hazard control.

Administration is a control that can easily be remembered by thinking, "This came from an office." Rules, regulations, policies, laws, training, posters, signs, and documents are all administrative controls.

Personal Protective Equipment (PPE) is the least effective control of all. PPE should always be considered the last resort of controlling a hazard. All you're really saying at this point is, "The best I can do to protect you is put some gear on you. Good luck." Sure, PPE is used as a baseline most of the time, but it is usually worn in conjunction with other controls further up the hierarchy.

Now that we have a clearer picture of the Hierarchy of Controls, let us return to our new-hire orientation. The controls in our scenario (OSHA policy, painted red line, company zero tolerance rule, posting signs every 15 feet) are all administrative controls. What if, instead of these administrative controls, we install a wall, hand rail, or some other fixed control to physically protect the employee from the hazard of falling, as opposed to simply bringing it to their attention and firmly suggesting they pay attention four different ways? One engineering control would exceed four combined administrative controls in effectiveness. Always using the hierarchy as it's designed will ensure you are using the best control available, thus making sure the employees are the safest they can be while performing the task.

That brings us to the A.L.A.R.P. principle.

A.L.A.R.P. stands for As Low As Reasonably Practicable (or in some circles, As Low As Reasonably Possible). The term stems from safety and risk-based methodology born in the UK in the 1970s. It is based on the idea that there is no such thing as zero risk, but rather risk falls onto a sliding scale of acceptability.

People employ this principle daily; for example, when driving to work. Are there any hazards between where you start your day and where you arrive at work? Of course there are hundreds, if not more. Yet at some point, you made the decision to make that drive anyway, despite the hazards. Why? Why purposefully put yourself in harm's way? I'm not talking about the monetary carrot we all follow to ensure our way of life. That's our motivator. What I'm asking is what made you feel safe enough to navigate those hazards, knowing that most of them would be there?

The answer is that all those controls from the hierarchy are working in harmony to make the risk as low as reasonably practicable.

For example, we undergo formal and informal driving training and education in order to attain a driver's license. (administrative controls). We have steering and braking mechanisms in our vehicles, so we can navigate around hazards and obstacles in our path (engineering controls). Traffic laws, roadside signs, and accepted driving courtesies ensure we know how to safely traverse the roadway (more administrative controls). If you ride a motorcycle, you might employ goggles, a helmet, and leather protective clothing (PPE). If you were accustomed to riding a bicycle but realized how exposed you were to hazards on your commute, you might decide driving your car would be a safer alternative (substitution control).

These controls have always been there, silently minimizing the risks and hazards which would otherwise impair your commute. Now, are the hazards gone? Did they up and disappear, leaving you to have a carefree trip with no other worry than which radio station to listen to? No. The hazards are still there, lying in wait to ruin your day, but the use of the most effective controls available provides a comfortable level of risk you accept on a daily basis.

Apply this same idea to the hazards on any job site. We utilize controls to drive down the level of risk, and using the best control available to ensure our employees' safety should be a best practice—perhaps the *only* practice.

We should train employees on how to use a saw properly instead of giving them gloves, eye protection, and wishing them luck (administrative vs. PPE). We should use a guard on the saw blade instead of telling employees to keep their hands out of the "danger zone" that is painted red (engineering vs. administrative).

What about eliminating the human exposure to the saw altogether? Impossible? I once observed an industrial miter saw set up to be pneumatically engaged by dual-activated palm controls on a pedestal located eight feet from the saw. The blade was guarded while in operation, and it had a braking mechanism on it which stopped the blade and retracted it once connection with either one of the palm buttons was broken. A light curtain activated the same braking and retraction system to ensure employees other than the operator could not gain access to the cutting area while the saw was in use. All these engineering controls eliminated human exposure. Elimination *is* possible.

Practicing this methodology moves us toward the result we all want in the first place: zero incidents.

INVERSION

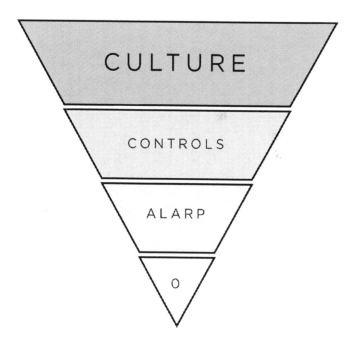

As we move through the levels of the Inverted Pyramid, we arrive at a completely different point than with the traditional Safety Pyramid.

Instead of arriving at a fatality, we arrive at the best place to achieve zero incidents.

Before we examine the Behavioral Formula in Part II, give these questions some thought:

- Are you proactive or reactive?
- Do you supervise or lead?
- Is your organization compliance-driven or excellence-driven?
- Are you still attempting to control the behavior of your employees?
- Where is your Outrage Meter currently calibrated to go off?
- What do you formally do to create a shift in employee behavior?
- Have you recognized the need for a change?

PART II

PERSPECTIVE AND THE BEHAVIORAL FORMULA: MAKING THE CHANGE

5

Exposure and Influence: The Birthplace of Perception

RARELY DO TWO PEOPLE SEE THE WORLD in the exact same way. People pull from their experiences and backgrounds to interpret and digest the circumstances they are faced with on a specific and individual basis.

In my presentations, I often invite people to discreetly name, in their opinion, the best restaurant and the best musician or musical group on a piece of paper. When they reveal their answers aloud, the concept of individuality hits with full force. While there are sometimes duplicate answers, most participants don't agree with each other, and sometimes they list obscure preferences nobody else has heard of. Allowing people to be simply themselves will expose how different we all are, based on nothing more than predetermined exposure and influence. If these individual differences exist in your employees outside of work, then wouldn't the same be true *at* work?

When I arrived at Fort Leonard Wood, MO for basic training in the summer of 2000, I found myself in a cocktail of different personalities. The people in my barracks formed a microcosm of the bigger picture. We hailed from New Mexico, Texas, Illinois, Michigan, and Wisconsin. Our ancestry was Irish, Italian, Hispanic, Scandinavian, and African. Some were tall and thick, others short and thin. City folk and country boys. Snow barons and desert rats. Ages ranged from 17 to 20. We were about as different as different gets.

We didn't get along at first. But in time, we became as close as brothers. That's how we ended up seeing each other. The same can be said for the folks I served with in Iraq. Not a single day goes by that I don't miss them, and I would still give my life it meant saving one of theirs. It is truly a different culture, but we didn't start that way.

The common ground all employees share is their humanity. It is the central element that sweeps all differences aside and gets all those links of chain melted down and re-poured into equal components of the culture. The life we are working for and supporting with our earnings may look different from the people to our left and right. (An employee once told me all he was going home to was his goldfish Bob.) But it is important enough and is loved enough to channel the need to sustain it, otherwise we wouldn't even be there.

So, how do you focus on an employee's humanity in a way that establishes the foundation of a safety culture?

I've had great success with implementing a "Safety Expectations" presentation as part of the new-hire orientation. It is an introduction to the culture, and nothing more. It establishes where the bar is set, along with a detailed explanation of why it is set so high, and a step-by-step layout of the expectations of each employee's individual responsibility as it relates to that culture. Yes, the orientation eventually includes presentations that go into the do's and don'ts, policies, regulations, and safety protocols on the compliance end of things. But defining the organization's behavioral expectations and its focus on culture and individual buy-in should be emphasized as a stand-alone message.

You only get one chance to make a first impression. If we are talking about protecting and sustaining our chosen livelihoods, preserving our way of life, and ensuring survival to enjoy those things, we should make the absolute best first impression we possibly can.

I rolled out this program to a manufacturing company that had 24 facilities around the United States. I was the EHS Manager for one of the 24 sites. Because this was a personalized program I had developed, our location was the only one formally participating.

About the time I began my second year there, a new plant manager was brought in. During his first week onsite, he brought in the senior management team members one at a time for an official meet-and-greet in his office.

In my meeting, he said, "Brian, I have one question for you. I've been looking into some trend data, comparing this operation with the others, and there is something happening here that I can't explain." He thumbed through a file folder and produced some printouts, dressed up with bright colored circles and arrows. "Out of every plant in North America, this operation has the lowest incident rate among new hires and contractors, which my experience and industry norms tell me should be the highest demographic for incidents. Can you explain that?"

There was only one thing we were doing differently, and I told him what it was.

He was skeptical that a one-hour presentation had the power to create a cultural shift big enough that it bucked company and industrial trends. But then he attended one. He walked away convinced that formally setting cultural expectations can make a difference.

Why do we need to formalize the emphasis on the cultural expectations? Isn't it apparent through the rest of the safety orientation how important safety is to the organization? Isn't what the culture stands for obvious on its own merit? That is a dangerous assumption too many companies make. If we want quantifiable results, we need to first clearly explain what we expect.

Years ago, I went through the training to become a certified ATV Safety Course Instructor. I learned to conduct classes to teach people how to safely operate all-terrain vehicles, also known as four-wheelers. The Master Instructor taught us to always assert authority. Not in an arrogant way, but to always communicate in such a way that your class participants know you are in ultimate control of the class and their actions, eliminating the chance for a misunderstanding that could eventually lead to an accident.

During one training demonstration, we were outside on the ATVs, and our instructor was a simulated class participant. I, as the simulated instructor, was to have my students exit to the perimeter of the training track one at a time, one behind the next, until they were all riding in a circle. I explained to the first student what I wanted, then told the rest of the group to exit to the perimeter one at a time when I said, "Go." I felt I gave a thorough explanation.

As the first student entered the perimeter track, the next student, our instructor, was supposed to follow. Instead, he went in the opposite direction, toward what would be a potential head-on collision with the first student. I panicked and shut down the exercise.

When I asked my instructor why he had deviated from my instruction, he reminded me that all I had told him to do was exit to the perimeter, not which direction to go.

He was right. I had given thorough instructions to the first student, then assumed everyone else would follow suit. Point taken.

Consider this: if the objective of a relay team is to win the race, whose leg of the race is most important? The answer: all of them. If the first leg does a great job, but leg two drops the baton, who fails? The whole team loses together, even the third and fourth legs that never got a chance to run. This demonstrates the importance of who we put into leadership roles, because they will be the ones held responsible for the passing of the baton.

How well are you communicating exactly what is it you want? Have clear expectations been established? Since people all see the world through their own lenses based on their earlier exposures and influences, getting the results you want requires clear, concise communication.

6

Perception: The Truth (Or Is It?)

I ONCE VISITED A TOURIST ATTRACTION in Texas that touted itself as a museum of the odd and bizarre. Inside the building, I followed a maze-like pathway to the first exhibit which showed a looping video on a television screen. It displayed images of people demonstrating the various ways they could twist, roll, and contort their tongues. A mirror placed near the screen invited guests to try and mimic the activity of the televised tongue charmers. I tried my hand (or tongue) at it, and I failed miserably to replicate what I saw. I laughed at myself and went on my way.

When the tour was nearly over, and I was on my way to the exit, it looked like there was one more exhibit to see. When I walked up to it, I got a sudden dose of perspective. It was the other side of the cleverly disguised two-way mirror from the first display. Standing before me, inches away, were idiots trying to mimic the tongue movements they saw on the TV screen next to them. I laughed at their naivety. But I stopped laughing when I remembered I had been one of the idiots just a few moments earlier.

Always take time to invest in perspective. I use the word *invest* here specifically and carefully, because it pays off. Taking a few moments to press pause, step outside the box, and do a complete walk-around of the situation and view it from different angles allows you to gain information that will help you process and interpret the situation better than just taking it at face value.

When people say, "Perception is reality," they mean that what somebody perceives to be the truth, whether it is or not, will be the basis of their actions. I agree, but I use a slight variation: "Without communication, and without clarification, perception is reality." I believe perception is closer to reality when people have an opportunity to investigate, analyze, clarify, and accept (or question) information based on their findings.

Consider Plato's *Allegory of the Cave*. Plato asks that you imagine being born into darkness. It is what you know as your reality. When you become conscious enough to be aware of it, you realize you are facing a wall and bound by chains, as are others on both sides of you. Occasionally, you are visited by images on the wall, moving and dancing in front of you. They come and go without rhyme or reason.

One day, you break your chains and wander into the recesses of this dark chamber. As you stumble along, you find a crackling, light-emitting, warmth-projecting mound on the floor. As you move, a darker portrayal of your movements is broadcast on the wall. As you move, it moves. You realize this is how the images you saw on the wall were created. You realize that the images on the wall weren't real things at all, but that something else made those movements. The images were only the byproduct of reality. Shadows.

Near this bright, dancing wonder at your feet is a ladder extending upwards. You pull yourself up, one rung at a time. Light begins to spill into the darkness from above. At the top, you step out and behold a whole new world of strange, wonderful things. The light stings your eyes, the air hurts your lungs, but it's beautiful, all of it.

As you reflect on your recent discoveries, you feel a paradigm shift. What you knew to be reality wasn't the only version that existed. The reality in the cave, enclosed by darkness, restraint, diversion, and misdirection kept you distracted from an alternative, more rewarding existence. Your ignorance of it didn't mean that it didn't exist; you simply hadn't discovered it yet.

You rush back down into the cave to tell the others what you found. As you elaborate with passion and detail the opportunities that await above, they grow angry and remind you that this—the darkness, the wall, the immobility—*this* is reality. They say you'd best get your head out of the clouds and accept it.

Appalled by their rejection, but encouraged by your new perspective, you leave them, and go to your new reality.

How does your organization compare to this situation? Is what the employee perceives to be factual indeed the case? Do you ever bother to ensure clarity takes place, or do you walk away assuming it did, much like I did on the ATV track? Does your culture teach accepting shadows as reality, or exploring opportunities for improvement as the best practice? Again, without communication, and without confirmation, perception becomes their reality.

Where does "common sense" fit into industrial safety and risk management? When should an employee just *know* something is true and what is the best way to behave?

I believe common sense is created by our Behavioral Formula. That is how we arrive at the beliefs and corresponding behaviors we consider common.

Far too often I hear people rely on the common-sense argument to explain away misunderstandings and gaps in communication. It usually sounds something like, "He should have known that. It's common sense!" Common to whom? You and others who experienced the same exposures and influences you did? What does that do to guarantee that every other person involved equally understood, and that it made sense to them?

I once investigated a safety incident that on the surface appeared to be a lockout/tagout violation. The operator of a large industrial saw had gotten into an electrical panel and manipulated a faulty wiring connection which had been shutting down the saw. The operator did this to keep the saw (and production) going.

Common sense suggests this employee should have known better, especially since she had exposed herself to high voltage and displayed extreme negligence for the sake of production. But one glaring thing stuck out to me. How did the saw operator, who spoke broken English and was not a certified electrician nor an instrumentation professional, know specifically how to fix the problem, not only knowing how to get into the cabinet, but also the specific set of wires to manipulate?

I asked the operator, who gave me a startling answer: "A maintenance guy showed me."

When I interviewed the maintenance tech, he vehemently denied doing so.

The problem I faced was an interesting one: I believed both of them.

Eventually, I pieced together what really happened. The operator had noticed the issue with the saw and told the shift lead, who in turn contacted the maintenance department to send someone to check it out.

When the maintenance tech arrived, he did his troubleshooting procedure and discovered a faulty wiring housing for the light curtain, a safety device that would signal the saw to disengage if an invisible light beam was interrupted. To demonstrate his discovery to the saw operator, he pointed out how when he jostled the wires to the light curtain, it resolved the problem. He had commented, "Here's your problem right here. See what happens when I do this? It fixes the problem. I just need to fix this, and we'll be back in business." The maintenance tech made notes to go to the warehouse to retrieve the parts to fix the problem, and he told the operator to take a break.

The operator, who was under the impression the maintenance tech had just shown her how to fix the problem herself, went back to business as usual. When the error happened again, the operator found the wires, jostled them until the problem corrected itself, and went back to work. This was the activity that was observed and reported as the safety violation.

Although there were many contributing factors that occurred in this case, it is undeniable that the operator's perception became a dangerous reality due to a breakdown in communication. If communication had been clear, we would not even be discussing this event. When it was made clear to the operator that she was exposing herself to a high voltage, and that a simple wrong move could have killed her, her face went white. She ran to the restroom and became physically ill.

Keep that in mind next time you want to label something as "common sense".

7

Thought:
Better Understanding through
Effective Communication

WHENEVER I WAS INVOLVED in incident investigations, after getting the high-level emergency stuff settled, I began the process by asking three questions about the employees involved:

1. How would the employee have known what to do?
2. Who would have told them how to do it properly?
3. What does that look like?

If I was unable to definitively answer all three questions, I could usually conclude that management and leadership had dropped the ball. The rest of the investigation simply turned into a fact-finding mission to determine how and where the failure occurred.

One time I was doing a project at home, and I took my youngest son along to be my "gopher". When I needed a Phillips screwdriver, I sent him to get one. After ten minutes of waiting, I got frustrated and went looking for him, angry that he was taking so long for a simple errand. This was, after all, why I had him with me, and I wouldn't have bothered if I had known he would goof off and not take the task seriously.

I found him in the garage. He sat in a pile of tools on the floor, picking up one screwdriver at a time, looking at it, and placing it down.

I asked, "Son, *what* are you doing?"

His face showed concern and frustration. "Dad, *none* of these screwdrivers say Phillips on them!"

While this is a cute story that paints the picture of perception vs. reality, these same circumstances can create grave results in the workplace. The primary takeaway here is how we need to reflect on where the breakdown happened. My son did exactly what he was asked to do. He did not deviate from his direction. He was not lazy, distracted, complacent, or trying to get out of doing work. He was attempting to do precisely what he was told, pulling from his own **exposures** and **influences** to inform his **perception** of what he **thought** it was that I asked for. He applied action to bring his **belief** and understanding of my request to life.

When the actual result ended up with

incorrect **behavior**, my initial reaction was to be angry and disappointed, and to assign blame. I assumed he deserved discipline, because I gave him specific instructions on what I wanted, and he failed to perform.

But once I had all the facts and refined my perspective, it was easy to see where things went awry. *I* was what went wrong. I did not set him up for success with his task. I assumed he knew what I wanted, but I had never taught him. Shame on me.

When handling employees, we are quick to assign blame, slow to gather perspective, and usually fail to refine our perspective. In analyzing this "incident", let's use the three questions for employees:

1. **How would he have known what to do?** He might have known about the difference between a Phillips and a flathead screwdriver if he been taught that before. Without that crucial information, it's hard to see a different outcome unless he made a lucky guess.

2. **Who would have told him how to do it properly?** This one falls squarely on the supervisor: me. Maybe he could have picked up the information from another source, such as a grandparent, an aunt or uncle, or TV. But that is an assumption I shouldn't have relied on. He was working for me, and any instruction on the project

should have come straight from me. Anything I left out would require interpretation, which is ruled by exposure, influence, and perception.

3. **What does that look like?** This would have taken the form of a simple hands-on explanation to describe what I may or may not need as tools for the task, including the dreaded Phillips screwdriver at the heart of our case. I was educated and knowledgeable about the task. I was *the* competent person. It was my responsibility to ensure adequate training took place for everyone involved.

Answering these questions ahead of time, proactively, would have prevented the situation from developing into a case study. If we systematically comb through the processes in our workplaces that create a potentially hazardous situation for our employees, ensure we are proactively answering these three questions with unequivocal clarity *before* an incident occurs, and then ensuring a formal answer exists *before* we expose employees to the potential risk, then we won't need to ask them *after* the fact nearly as often.

Clear, concise, effective communication helps transform thoughts into belief.

In my training sessions, I have an exercise that helps emphasize the importance of this matter. I begin by telling the participants that there are a few simple rules that must be followed. First, they must keep their eyes on their own papers. Next, there mustn't be any verbal interaction between me and them, aside from my giving them instructions on what I would like them to do. Here are my instructions, given in about a 20-second window:

1. Draw a square.
2. Quadrisect your square.
3. Number your quadrants algebraically, using Roman Numerals.
4. Around the outside of Roman Numeral one, draw a star.
5. Around Roman Numeral two, draw a hexagon.
6. Around Roman Numeral three, draw an arrow pointing east.
7. Around Roman numeral four, draw an arrow pointing south.
8. Stop and put your pencils down.

Many participants give up around the third or fourth instruction. At the end, I reveal the diagram I intended for them to make:

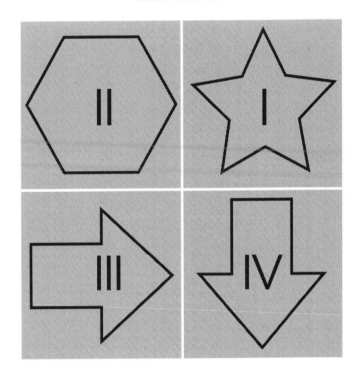

Next, I invite them to share their results with their neighbors. As the laughter and chatter about individual interpretations of my instructions fill the room, I bring them all back to Earth with a harrowing revelation: they all heard the exact same words, from the same person, in the same room, at the same time. Not only did they draw something different from what I asked for, but they didn't even get what each other got. How is that even possible?

In all fairness, was I intentionally aloof with my instructions? Was I purposefully vague? Did I use terms and language that were sure to create confusion? Absolutely.

I remind them to reflect on what it was I took away from them at the beginning of the exercise: the ability to communicate. By revoking the opportunity to ask questions, seek clarification, or slow my instructions, I ensured their failure. This exercise, and ones like it, raise the question: how effective are we when we communicate with each other? A great follow-up question is: how often can a workplace incident be blamed on poor communication?

By taking into consideration that we all draw from our own individual exposures and influences to interpret a set of circumstances presented to us, we can truly see how easy it is for a failure to occur. The only way to successfully transform thought into belief is with clear, concise communication.

8

Belief: Better Decision-Making

TAKE A MOMENT to think about the things you believe. Now ask yourself why you believe them. Odds are, the progression of your exposure, influence, perception, and thought over your lifetime have informed your current beliefs. Now, consider what it would take to get you to believe otherwise. What would get you to change your mind and believe the opposite of your current stance?

As an example, take a pen and clasp it between the thumb and index finger of your dominant hand, and hold it straight up-and-down for the remainder of the exercise. Lift the pen over your head so you're looking straight up at it. Still holding it straight up-and-down, begin making small, clockwise circles as though you are drawing them on the ceiling. As you look up, ask yourself if you truly believe those are clockwise circles.

The answer should be a resounding *yes*. You

are, after all, in control of this situation and creating the motion yourself. Of course they are clockwise circles, no question. Now, slowly lower the pen. Keep it straight up-and-down and do not alter the direction of your circles. Keep lowering the pen until you are looking down at the tip instead of upward at its base.

What direction are those circles going now? Somehow, mysteriously, the circles have started going in the opposite direction: counterclockwise. What just happened?

The reason I was so specific about the pen orientation and the direction of the circles was to create a sterile, controlled exercise by eliminating circumstantial influence. You remained in control of the pen and the circular action from beginning to end, yet you were ready to change your belief to the complete opposite answer by the end of the exercise.

Why?

Perspective.

Companies must realize they are not inheriting blank slates when it comes to their employees' mindsets. Companies are competing with everything that created the current set of beliefs in every single person. The reasons why a person believes something do not go away, and unless there is a meaningful event to change that trajectory, why would anyone suddenly discontinue their current way of believing? Like an arrow in flight, belief won't deviate from its course on its own.

Considering the diverse belief systems that we know exist within every one of our employees, it appears as though there are three options for attaining the culture we desire. The first option is to completely reprogram the person's individual Behavioral Formula, essentially restarting the entire process and controlling the exposures and influences so the person arrives at the mindset we want. This would require a sterile environment and a single-minded sense of dedication to the cause for it to work. The only entities that can reset a person's formula like this are organizations with the budget, timeline, and resources to create a revitalized, finished product in the person, such as the military and professional sports teams. Your business probably lacks such extensive resources and time.

The second option is to let the employee slowly soak in the workplace culture and hope that over time they will absorb the sense of what is right and wrong, safe and unsafe, on their own. While they will no doubt be exposed to the desired cultural elements in the form of training videos, safety committees, company policies and procedures involving safety protocols, and gimmicks designed to draw attention to participating in safe work practices, they will still be mostly driven by the belief system they brought with them. Their individual buy-in to the stimuli around them hinges largely on those pre-established beliefs and whether they mesh with the ideologies of the culture. If they are compatible, you might have what appears to be a good fit and gain an employee who exhibits acceptable behavior. If they don't align, you get a person who will come across as countercultural, not bought-in, and a weak link in your cultural chain. Most companies take this approach, whether they realize it or not. They believe the employee will come to terms on his own accord, and if not, the employee will weed himself out.

This is a dangerous approach.

Employees who are left to figure things out on their own simply find ways to become comfortable in a system that does not hold them accountable until it's too late. If their belief system has not changed, why would they act any differently?

Suppose you were put into a room filled with memorabilia for a band belonging to a genre of music that you don't like. While the band's music is being pumped through the speakers hanging from the ceiling, you notice a collection of other kinds of music available for play, including some selections from your favorite band. What would probably happen first: changing the music to your own preference, or slowly become a fan of the music that you are obviously being pressured to listen to? Similarly, employees will default to their own preferences if they are left to make an independent judgement call.

That brings us to option three, which involves providing a sudden change so jarring that it creates an internal paradigm shift from that point on. An employee's belief system is shocked into considering of an alternative way of thinking. Perspective is the most effective tool we have for building a culture, largely because of the impact it can have on a person's belief system.

Picture someone who grows up on a small island being taught their entire life that what the rest of the world knows to be the color green is red, and vice versa. Now remove that person from the island and drop them into any metropolis in the world. They quickly become aware that their point of view is different from everyone around them. It will be confusing and frustrating to learn that the entire world is backwards and doesn't know one color from the other.

Over time, this person comes to terms with the fact that *they* were misinformed, and *they* were the anomaly, even though it was already crystal clear to everyone else. But before that personal revelation occurred, were they wrong? Maybe in a strictly factual sense they were, but consider it from their point of view. Were they being neglectful, or forgetful? Were they being malicious with disregard? Did they deviate from what they had been told and trained to believe?

Once again, it's always a best practice to consider perspective.

Compare this hypothetical situation with a post-incident root cause analysis and investigation. What would your conclusion be? The employee was misinformed? They were not trained appropriately? They were mistaken, and due to inappropriate exposure, they misunderstood? If that was your conclusion, what would your corrective or preventative actions be? Better training? A more thorough screening before having the employee perform the task in the first place?

But we are asking all this *after* the incident, which puts us back on the wrong side of the Safety Pyramid discussion. Scary how quickly that happens, isn't it?

Many organizational perception surveys show a vast difference between what hourly employees believe and what the executives believe is the current state of the company safety culture. How is it that people working for the same organization under the same guidelines, policies, and procedures end up on such different ends of the spectrum? Perhaps the answer isn't so far out of reach.

What do you currently do to transform the way your employees think and believe?

- How do you account for the humanity your employees built over a lifetime and bring with them to work?

- Are you relying on mind-numbing training that simply tells employees a bunch of things they need to do to be compliant, so you can keep regulatory agencies at bay?
- Do you refer the employees to a dictionary-sized manual, then have them acknowledge they read it and understand the contents with a flick of their pen?
- What is the employees' perception of the safety program and what it's about, including the intent of the company officials charged with its administration?
- Do you consider certain employees to be incapable of understanding the importance of safety, finding it better to shrug in frustration and hope for the best?
- Have you considered that your workers are people first, and employees second?
- Are you still under the impression that you can control your employees' behavior?

9

Behavior: Better Choices

THE LAST STOP ON OUR WAY TO CULTURE is the place where many companies misguidedly start: behavior. Human behavior is the largest component of workplace culture. It is present in every person who walks through the door. It is simultaneously the most important aspect of the culture, and potentially the most detrimental. Attempting to control it may seem like the logical thing to do, but remember: you simply can't control human behavior.

The closest we can come to controlling human behavior in the workplace is restricting it. This usually looks like policies, procedures, guidelines, and disciplinary action for not abiding by these rules (administrative controls). But like stored energy, human behavior still exists in its natural state within the confines of these restrictions. It is simply contained for a limited time, and given the chance to release, it will reassume its natural form. A tiger in a cage is still a tiger. Once the cage is opened, the tiger will simply go back to doing tiger things.

This is why so many workplace incidents occur when the supervisor or safety representative is not present. When nobody is looking, an employee will revert to pre-existing behaviors. The pressure to conform to the restrictions has been removed, and now all that remains is the natural behavior. When an incident occurs under these circumstances, it isn't so much that an employee deviated from their training or made a conscious choice to not comply with the rules. Instead, they never really bought into the cultural ideology that the rules represent in the first place. They only played along because they were told they "had to". As soon as they felt like they didn't "have to" anymore, for whatever reason, they dropped the charade and reverted to what was more natural and more comfortable.

On the other hand, some employees may appear to be "safety minded" or bought-in, even with no formal exposure to safety principles through the company. They simply behave in a way that is natural to them based on their Behavioral Formula.

This is why we must acknowledge our employees' humanity, not suppress it. Just like when we are asked to name our favorite restaurants and musicians, we all default to our own humanity that has taken shape over a long time. If an individual has no intention of buying into the culture, then no amount of attempted suppression will allow you to control the outcome. Not your attorney-drafted disclaimer in your employee handbook. Not your OSHA-compliant safety program. Not the professionally edited safety video library you show to employees. Not the number of days without a lost-time accident proudly displayed on the wall. Not your credentialed safety staff.

I simply don't believe that using control as a control for behavioral development is effective.

Some of my colleagues believe that managing workplace safety through the implementation of systems and tools is a preferred and more effective method than emphasizing the behavioral aspects of the business culture. Their stance is not without merit. It is true that without the proper tool for the job, and without a formal system to ensure proper functionality, the employee is largely set up for failure. I have worked for several organizations that were ISO and OHSAS Management System certified for safety, environment, and quality. I've served as an internal auditor of the OHSAS 18001 system. I am quite familiar with the benefits of management systems, and I advocate for their use where the elements can realistically be used and sustained.

My expanded take is simply this: are these not controls? A management system, even one that is world-class, is just a high-functioning administrative control.

I'm also a firm believer in using the best and most appropriate tool for the job. (This is also a compliance mandate.) But the best tool money can buy is just an engineering control waiting to be used as intended by the employee.

Here's another way to look at it. Let's say you have a new guitar. It has the finest trim, is made with the best wood, is strung with premium strings, and is perfectly tuned. With your new guitar comes custom sheet music and tablature written by the world's finest guitarists. You also have in hand a catalogue of lyrics penned by the most soulful poets and lyricists around. While you now have everything you physically need to make a studio-quality recording that might be worth millions, most people would find themselves unable to do much more than make noise that would go no further than the Deleted Items folder. What was neglected to be brought into focus in this scenario was the very essence of what makes music come to life: the musician. Ability and emotional harmony between the player and the instrument create the music, not the instrument or the notes on the sheet alone. The same can be said for the singing of the lyrics. Without inflection and emotion, they are just words.

When aligned behavior is married to the right system and the proper tools, it is a harmonious coupling. Each can exist independently of the other, much like single notes in a scale, but when played together in harmony, the chord rings out and realizes its true potential.

What can't be ignored is that the Behavioral Formula and the opportunity to interject perspective lies upstream of every control you put into place, and the effectiveness of the control lies in the hands of those who use it. For a system or tool to work properly, an employee must use it the way it was designed to be used, right? So, what is ensuring the employee's buy-in? What assurance do you have that they understand the value of what the system or tool is intended to accomplish, and do they embrace what their personal contribution looks and feels like?

It's easy to believe that you can develop a program for occupational safety by controlling people's behavior, but it's a pipedream. The focus should always be on finding a way to effectively *change* the behavior, not control it. That way, the employee behaves in a way conducive to the culture because they *want* to, not because they're told they must. The best way to do that is by using perspective.

What does it look like for somebody to have a trajectory change in their belief system, and therefore their behavior, due to nothing more than perspective?

My army unit was deployed to Baghdad, Iraq

in the spring of 2004 to support infrastructure rebuilding. Not that there was ever a good time to be there, but that certainly wasn't one. There were many long, dark stretches of time when all we really wanted to do was just go home. Many of us got through those times by daydreaming during our down time about what we might like to do once we got back to the U.S. and got out of the military. One guy wanted to go home to work in the steel mills in Pennsylvania. Another guy wanted to go be a beach bum in Florida. As for me, growing up in a mining town in rural New Mexico, and now having five years of explosives experience under my belt, I figured I would be a shoo-in for the blasting crew at the mine.

A year and a half later, I found myself heading to my first day of work at the mine. Because the mine I worked at was a surface operation, MSHA (Mine Safety and Health Administration) mandated that all new miners receive 24 hours of training spread out over three eight-hour days. The first morning, I walked into that class feeling on top of the world. Nobody was shooting at me anymore. I could just punch the clock, do my job, go home, and relax. Life had a very rosy glow that morning.

As I took my seat, I noticed a man standing in the front of the class by himself. He wasn't talking with anyone but was dressed like he might be someone important. When the class started, the instructor introduced this man. He was the President of Mining Operations, and I assumed he was there to do the "presidential" thing: welcome us to mining, to the operation, to the class.

I was wrong. He was there to tell us a story. Only days before, he had the unfortunate responsibility of going to the home of an employee who had been killed on the job, and notifying the family. At first, I thought this was a scare tactic, a fabricated story told to get a group of new hires to pay attention "or else". But it quickly became apparent that wasn't the case.

His cautionary tale, while sorrowful, was digestible and tolerable, until he brought up the little boy. He told us he was trying to break the tragic news in a mild version because he couldn't bring himself to come right out and tell the boy exactly what happened. As he was searching for words and thoughts that didn't exist, the little boy asked, "What do you mean, mister? Where did he go? What do you mean he's not coming home? Where's my daddy?"

That's where he lost it.

He wept in front of us all. He made his final statements and solemnly excused himself. In the palpable silence that followed, a singular thought kept running through my mind over and over again: *When does it end*? I thought I left all that behind me when I exited military service. I had been certain I didn't need to worry ever again about dying while doing my job, or worry about losing my friends and coworkers. Sure, I'd imagined plenty of times that someone might deliver that message to my family, but it always looked like two uniformed soldiers saying, "We regret to inform you..." It never occurred to me I could still get severely injured or die at work.

It hit me hard because I had sons the same age as the boy in the story. Imagining they might hear the message from someone they didn't know, a stranger explaining that I didn't come home because of a preventable accident—especially after surviving the hell of combat, it was just unbearable. That morning, my rose-colored glasses slipped off my nose and shattered on the floor.

In my career in occupational safety and health, I've had the privilege of instructing, teaching, consulting, and mentoring thousands of people. I've conducted seminars and presentations for dozens of industries in as many places. I acquired a college degree and a pocket full of certifications and accolades for various accomplishments in the field. I've written articles and essays in an effort to reach others and share my thoughts and beliefs on safety and workplace excellence. I am driven by an unyielding passion, devoted to an ideal bigger than I am as an individual, and have somehow figured out how to make a living from it.

None of this would have come to pass if it were not for hearing that story that morning. My entire career in health and safety was launched that day.

So, if you still wonder if it is possible to change a person's behavior through nothing but perspective, look no further. You're holding the answer in your hands.

10

Refined Perspective:
The Risk of Assumption

PERSPECTIVE IS LIKE climbing out of Plato's cave and seeing something new for the first time. But new information doesn't always make sense, and it can appear to contradict our current knowledge. It is much easier to default to what we think we already know, especially when new information seems unlikely or counterintuitive. Recognizing when this happens—and fighting the urge to accept circumstances as they appear to be—is an important factor in risk management, and a fundamental exercise when considering a perspective-based safety culture. I call this "Refined Perspective".

Refined Perspective is the antithesis of assumption. Instead of assuming, we must train ourselves to discover. When we do this, we uncover elements of a situation that may cause us to reconsider our position.

One morning during my time working in the

mining industry, the Safety Department got a call from the Environmental Department informing us there had been an ammonium nitrate spill at the blasting agent loading area. The surface mines used ANFO (short for Ammonium Nitrate mixed with Fuel Oil) for the blasting operations, because it is extremely effective at fracturing rock. The spilled material was captured within the secondary containment, so Environmental had no further commitment to the situation; but Safety needed to go inspect and clear the area, so the material owner could clean it up safely.

My boss called me and said, "Owens! You did explosives in the military, right?"

I said, "Yes, ma'am."

"Alright," she said, "this one's yours. Get to the blasting agent storage area."

There was a concrete containment area with three large tanks inside its barrier walls. The first two tanks were clearly labeled with a placard identifying the contents as being an oxidizer, which ammonium nitrate is. The third tank didn't appear to have any labeling at all, which was an issue in and of itself, but not directly related to this event and something I could simply add to my report notes for a subsidiary corrective action.

It seemed that an ammonium nitrate delivery tanker was in the process of unloading its contents into the middle tank when it suddenly began overflowing. This was discovered to be due to a faulty tank volume gauge. By the time the driver shut off the pump, there were about two inches of ammonium nitrate in the basin of the containment area and around the bases of the other tanks.

By itself, ammonium nitrate is just fertilizer. It needs the addition of diesel fuel oil and an adequate initiator before it becomes dangerous. All I was seeing at this point was one side of the hazard triangle. I wasn't overly concerned about an intensified situation developing, as long as the cleanup process eliminated the introduction of a second (and most especially a third) side of the triangle, such as diesel fuel oil. I was about to release the area for cleanup when I heard a big rig downshift and slow down behind me. I turned to see a diesel tanker slowing as if to turn into our location.

The driver pulled up alongside me and parallel to the tanks. He got out of the cab and lumbered toward me. "Hey," he said, "I don't mean to bother y'all, but is it alright if I go ahead and unload into the tank?"

I said, "No, sir. These are ammonium nitrate tanks. In fact, I need you to clear out of here immediately."

He pointed to the unlabeled tank. "No, no, *that* tank."

"*No*," I reiterated, "that's an ammonium nitrate tank, too."

"Nope, that's a diesel tank. I've been

unloading here for years."

I looked at the tank, then back at him. "Stay right there. Don't do a thing."

He gave me a sloppy salute soaked in sarcasm.

I examined every inch of the tank. As I walked around the back side, my attention was drawn to some faint, sun-faded letters that were barely discernable.

DIESEL.

Suddenly, I had a different understanding of the danger of the situation.

But that understanding only happened after I took a deeper look at what I thought I already knew. It wasn't that I had faulty information or that I was misinformed. No, I was confident that I had all the information I needed to make a sound decision. My problem was that I allowed *logic* to overrule my search for *confirmation*. It never occurred to me that someone would intentionally store an oxidizer and a combustible in large quantities side-by-side in the same containment area.

My military training and education (my exposure and influence) led me to the dreaded place of defaulting to "common sense". I took the missing placard on the tank to be an administrative oversight, not the fundamental piece of investigative information it truly was. To learn that it had been that way for so many years without anybody understanding it was a potentially disastrous arrangement may have left me awestruck, but it also gifted me with something far more valuable: the appreciation of Refined Perspective.

Assumption often leaves us with a familiar, comfortable point of view. In some areas of life, this is benign. But the consequences of assumptions in an industrial setting can be dire. Assumptions breed opportunities for disaster.

I investigated another incident that left me with a life-long hatred for assumption. An electrical contractor had come in to replace light ballasts in four identical, adjacent rooms. There were parallel hallways on either side of these rooms, with doors leading out into each hallway. One of the hallways housed the breaker box supplying the power to the rooms, and also where the electricians performed their lockout/tagout for this task.

According to policy, the electricians also needed to perform a tryout, or a controlled verification to ensure that what they had de-energized was indeed off before they proceeded. This involved using a volt meter to test the wiring going into each ballast before the wire was cut to remove the old ballast. Room by room, ballast by ballast, these electricians performed their energy control responsibilities perfectly—that is, until they got to the last room.

It was the end of the day, everyone was tired, and none of them wanted to stay later than they needed to. They performed their lockout/tagout at the breaker box just like they'd done all day long. When they entered the room, the lights were out, and everything was dark, just like it was supposed to be. It was obvious that whoever had wired the room had done it right, ensuring that all the wiring for these rooms was fed from the same breaker box. They used the volt meter on the first ballast and found it to be neutralized, as expected.

Comfortable and confident, they skipped this step for the remainder of the ballasts, to save time. But when they cut into the last ballast in the room, they discovered it was still energized. As it turns out, that ballast was the only one fed from another breaker in the other hallway. As fate would have it, all four bulbs were burned out, adding to the illusion that everything was as it appeared to be.

I doubt I need to elaborate any more on why assumption has no place in any workplace safety culture.

11

Culture: X Marks the Spot

ACCEPTABLE CULTURAL OUTCOMES only become possible when people's individual Behavioral Formulas are similar, or when they have been affected by perspective that aligns their collective behavior. It takes 100% buy-in from everyone for it to work.

Archways are some of the longest-lasting man-made structures. Even when the rest of a building has long since fallen into ruin, the archway remains firmly intact. That is because by design, each piece holds the next in place. The strength comes from unity. But remove one piece of the arch, and it will crumble and fall. Likewise, without unified buy-in and commitment, our culture will fall apart as soon as it is put under strain.

We might be inclined to believe that everyone who does not buy in to the culture immediately is problematic, contrary, and needs to be terminated. While using the hiring process to screen for cultural incompatibility is a best practice, as is using fair disciplinary action to curb negligence, I've experienced some of my most profound professional encounters with these types of people.

I call them the "Hard Cases". They appear to be a detriment to the culture because of their behavior. They come across as stubborn, arrogant, unapproachable, nonmalleable, and in many other ways a hindrance to cultural development and sustainability. But before we pass judgment, let's ask: what made them that way? Have we looked at this person using Refined Perspective before making our final decision? Are they truly a weak link in the culture, or have they just not yet been given the proper dose of perspective?

One day I was in my office getting caught up on some paperwork, and a supervisor came in. He plopped down in an empty chair.

Seeing his woeful disposition, I asked, "What's up?"

He said, "Oh, I've got this kid on my crew, great worker, runs circles around everyone else. A real go-getter type, you know?"

"Sounds great. What's the problem?"

"I think I need to let him go."

I sat back in my chair and gave him my full attention. "Why's that?"

"I just can't get him bought into the idea of safety. I know he means well, but he's all about pushing through and getting the job done—"

"Even at the expense of his own safety," I said, finishing his sentence.

"Yeah." He sighed in frustration.

"Well, don't run him off just yet," I told him. "Let me have a try first."

He smiled and said, "I was hoping you'd say that."

About half an hour later I heard a light rap on my door. I looked up to see a young man, about 20 years old and partially hidden by the doorway. He was grimy and dusty.

"Come on in," I said. "Pull up a seat. What's going on?"

He drew a deep sigh, never taking his eyes off the floor at his feet. "I think I'm gonna get fired."

"What makes you say that?"

"I just get in trouble all the time for dumb safety rules. I don't mean to, I just..." His voice trailed off into solemn frustration.

"Go ahead," I assured him. "It's alright."

"They just—kind of get in the way of getting the job done. I've never worked somewhere with so many dumb safety rules! I have to fill out a form for every little thing, or do a half hour of preparation for a three-minute job. It just feels like such a waste of time!"

I asked, "What did you do before coming here?"

"I grew up on a ranch," he said. "We worked hard. Sunup to sundown, sometimes longer. I was brought up to put in an honest day's work and never had so many rules to follow. It's just hard."

"I understand," I said. "What are you so worried about this job for, anyway? You're young, I'm sure there's plenty of opportunity out there for a hard worker like you."

"Not like this," he said. "My wife and I just had a baby. This is a great job, and the benefits are really good."

I asked, "You got pictures?" This was the first time he and I locked eyes since he came in. "The family, you have pictures?"

With a shy smile, he nodded yes.

"Break 'em out, man!"

He took out his wallet and thumbed out some pictures. He handed me a photograph of him and his young bride at their wedding. The next photo showed an adorable baby girl who had her dad's blue eyes.

I said, "Tell me about them."

He went on to brag about the most precious parts of his life for the next ten minutes, glowing with pride.

When there was a natural lull in the conversation, I asked him, "Which way is your compass pointing?"

He furrowed his brow. "Pardon?"

I asked, "What do we use a compass for?"

He cautiously offered, "To point the way, help us keep direction, help us get where we're going."

"That's right," I said. "So, where is it you're trying to get to?"

His eyes fell on the pictures in his hands.

"You spend an awful lot of time here at work, performing tasks that can be pretty hazardous. If you're not doing the very best you can to work safely, aren't you allowing circumstances to dictate your direction?" I opened my desk drawer and pulled out a compass I knew was there. Sliding it across the desk to him, I said, "I'll ask you again. Where is your compass pointing, and are you sure you're going to get there?"

His jaw clenched, and his bottom lip quivered. A single tear ran through the dirt on his face. He didn't say another word, just nodded in understanding. He stood up, put the pictures back in his wallet, and wiped away the tear. He offered me his hand.

I shook it firmly and said, "Take that compass with you."

He tucked the compass into his jacket pocket and walked out the door.

Two weeks later, his supervisor drifted in and plopped down in the same chair. "What did you say to that kid?"

"Why, how's he doing?"

"Well, he hasn't lost a step with his work ethic, but now he's like a reborn safety champion or something. He's always the first to call someone out if they're not being safe, even the older guys. What did you tell him?"

I said, "I just gave him a compass."

"That reminds me," said the supervisor. "He wanted me to give this to you." He pulled out my compass and handed it back to me. "He wanted me to tell you he bought his own."

"Good man," I said, placing my compass back in the desk drawer.

The supervisor shook his head and stood to leave. "You safety guys are a strange bunch. I don't get it, but I appreciate what you did. It obviously worked."

Perspective has served me well since the earliest days of my career. On the morning of my first safety meeting as a brand-new safety professional, I had everyone huddle in the yard before heading out to work at the mine. It was a cold morning. Snow was on the ground, and I could see my breath as I gave my pre-shift lecture on the pursuit of zero incidents. I was rolling along like a preacher, loving the sound of my own voice, and feeling like I was changing the world with my passion.

Then a hand went up in the back of the crowd.

The hand belonged to a Hard Case who had been around for decades and didn't want to listen to a message about safety, let alone from a youngster still wet behind the ears.

I said, "Sir, do you have a question?"

"Yeah, I was just wondering if you really believe all that zero shit you're saying."

"As a matter of fact, I do. Don't you?"

"Naw," he drawled, "not really."

"Okay," I said. "I'll bite. Why not?"

"Look, kid, you gotta understand something. A lot of us, we've been around a long time. Seen a lotta things. Seen folks come and go—some in body bags. We ain't handing out tickets at the carnival. This is a dangerous job, and we know it. We do it anyway. Sure, working safe is a good idea, and we do the best we can, but that doesn't mean your zero is actually possible, cause it ain't, so you might as well wrap this up. We got work to do."

I was met with a quietness I will never forget. Everyone looked at me as if to say, "Whatcha got, Mr. Safety Man?"

I admit, I was on the spot in a big way. But I noticed the Hard Case wore an NFL team cap, so I decided to use perspective to make my point I said, "Let's look at it like this. Does a football team ever set foot on the field to lose?"

A few people muttered tongue-in-cheek comments about other people's favorite teams, and the chatter went around for a minute or two. But nobody offered me an argument.

I said, "So, let's talk about that. What does a team do to actively pursue losing?" Again, there were some mumbled jokes about keeping certain quarterbacks on the roster, but no one gave me a serious answer.

"Alright," I said. "What does a team do to

ensure a win?"

Suddenly, people spoke up with dozens things a football team does to win.

I asked, "Okay, so do we all agree that a team tries much harder to win than it does to lose?"

Everyone conceded the point.

I said, "In spite of all the things a team does to try to win, is it still the very real and unfortunate possibility that they're going to lose a game or two along the way?"

Everyone nodded yes, including the Hard Case.

"It's never the goal, never the intent, but yes, that is a real potential. But," I asked, "is it possible to have an undefeated season?"

My Hard Case's face broke into a smile, and his eyes shone with amusement. You see, he was wearing a Miami Dolphins ball cap. The Dolphins are the only NFL team to have an entirely undefeated season, from the opening game all the way to winning the Super Bowl.

That morning clued me into the power of perspective. It was about more than winning an argument with a Hard Case. The larger victory that morning was seeing the lightbulbs go on one at a time in the rest of the group.

That is why I do what I do. I could have lost thirty minds that morning, forever establishing that safety is just a bunch of talk from folks who learned fancy concepts in a textbook and have no sense of practical application. Instead, I firmly established a position of trust with a crew of Hard Cases, thanks to the timely use of perspective.

For the record, I never had another contest come up in a meeting again. But more importantly, not a single one of those people was injured during the remainder of my time at the company.

12

Zero: Life After the Change

ON OUR JOURNEY to finding a way to eliminate employee injuries through cultural development, we must also explore our own motivation. Why are we as business practitioners in today's industry compelled to pursue zero in the first place? After all, workers' compensation insurance is alive and well, and it is in place to provide a level of protection for the business against all numbers other than zero. Why burden our schedules with just another spinning plate on a stick we need to keep from falling? Isn't it much easier to take comfort in knowing there is a broom and dust pan in the closet to clean up the plate if it falls and breaks? If we can just go to the cupboard and grab another plate, why fret?

The reason that generally floats to the top is compliance. OSHA's mission statement charges all employers to "assure safe and healthful working conditions for working men and women by setting and enforcing standards and by providing training, outreach, education, and assistance." (MSHA has a similar position.) Since these are regulatory agencies with the power of enforcement, playing by the rules and committing to workers' safety as mandated by law is a powerful reason to stay as close to zero as possible.

The more practical reason to buy into the idea of zero is that it just makes good business sense. In addition to the fines that regulatory agencies can impose, the closer you can land to zero, the less money you pay out in direct costs. The less you pay out in direct costs, the less you pay out in indirect costs.

Workers' compensation is a nice insurance policy to have, but for many companies, their Experience Modifier will determine whether the business sinks or swims. The Experience Modifier is a number that, in part, represents the cost of past accidents and the likelihood of future accidents. (The company's payroll is part of the formula as well.) Insurance companies use this to set the cost of a company's workers' compensation premiums. If a company has too many injury claims, they end up with a monster of a premium to pay. Before they know it, they can no longer be competitive in their industry because the premiums are bleeding them dry. Self-insured companies are no better off. Their insurance payments come right out of the bottom line.

Many insurance companies offer premium discounts for having a formal safety program in place, as well as a positive trend history—another reason a good workplace safety culture is smart business. Dollars and cents go a long way to motivate business owners.

But the reason that hits closest to home for me is the human factor. When *people* are seen and addressed through the smokescreen of being an *employee*, it is easier to ask them to cut corners to increase or sustain production output. An employee is easily seen as a literal human *resource*, an expendable cog in the wheel of the industrial machine; and as with any machine, parts are simply replaced with new parts when necessary. But once we see those employees as people, it becomes much harder to ask such sinister favors.

If you are in a leadership role, think about some of the more questionable orders you may have given someone for the sake of production. Have you ever directly asked someone, or perhaps implied, they should cut a corner to maintain their pace? At the time, you might have dismissed it as a necessary risk for the greater good, and if nothing bad happened and the outcome was favorable, then you might have convinced yourself the risk was worth it. You might be inclined to do it again in the future.

Now replace the cast of this melodrama with your own loved ones. These are no longer faceless pawns, or employees you keep at arm's length. To you, these are the dearest members of the human race. Would you make the same request knowing it was your children who would be putting themselves in harm's way to complete the task? Would you be so quick to focus on the deadline, doing whatever necessary to meet it? Or would you take the time to consider whether the best possible controls are in place, and only then allow them to perform the task as safely as possible?

What if there was no time to do the necessary training for a task? Would you willingly send your wife or husband to perform that dangerous job?

Here's a wake-up call: your employees are the dearest members of the human race to *someone*, and your loved ones are (or will be) working for someone you hope will have their best interests in mind.

The stories and ideas in this book did not come without a cost. I have seen more industrial loss and occupational tragedy than anyone would ever care to, but those events led me to an important realization: if the incident number isn't zero, then it's another number. And if that number represents a person, who will it be? I dare you to put a face to that number, keeping firmly in mind that face belongs to a person, and that someone is counting on that person to return home exactly the way they were when they left for work. And if they don't, it happened on your watch.

The second you hire someone, you instantly accept their behavior as it is, and you become responsible for it while they're at work. Are you comfortable rolling the dice on their cultural buy-in, crossing your fingers that they absorb the stuff they need to be a good fit? If not, what are you doing to change it?

If we expect to create and sustain a culture based on the idea of nobody getting hurt on the job, we must:

1. Acknowledge that every employee is a person, and that the Behavioral Formula shaped them.

2. Understand that when we hire an employee, we are accepting their behavior as it is—contractually, legally, accepting.

3. Concede that there is no way to control that behavior, and that it was created by other factors, and that it predates their employment.

4. Understand that if we do try to restrict behavior, the employee's perceptions and beliefs will have more bearing on their decisions than the policy or rule telling them how you want them to behave.

5. Understand the power that perspective gives us. Finding opportunities to use it proactively and effectively can change the existing behavior, causing a trajectory

shift that hits the cultural mark.

6. Do this formally so we reach every single employee in the organization, creating a culture based on expectations grounded in quality and excellence.

Once we have established our cultural expectations, we are positioned to implement the remaining principles of Inversion. Culture is the first and most important piece in the Inverted Pyramid. Once we have company-wide buy-in, the remaining challenges become manageable.

The concepts in this book are just ideas, but as I mentioned earlier, ideas are the birthplace of action. Let's consider this the start of our relay race, and I have handed the baton to you. The success of the race now depends on forward momentum and a continued passing of the baton.

My hope for you is that you now see that your true investment wasn't in the acquisition of this collection of pages, but rather in your enlightenment due to the gift they provided within their folds. The gift my grandfathers and so many others gave me along the way.

The gift of perspective.

Acknowledgments

MANY PEOPLE have shaped my understanding of perspective and its value. I want to thank a few of them here: Stanley B., John O., Mr. G., Scotty J., Fred M., Dan G., Tim B., Melissa W., Rob M., Heidi S., Chino T., Joe E., Tony O., Chris P., Rick M., Jay K., Larry C., Alan B., Kevin C., Skip L., Lee W., Jack P., Brian P., Jason F., John B., Laura S., Luella W., Alex R., Aaron J., Steve M., my folks, Ashley O., and most of all, my family. There is no greater inspiration, no greater influence on my passion to serve, than you. You continue to give me every reason to stay true to my commitment to come home to you. I love you all dearly.

About the Author

B RIAN O. OWENS HAS A DIVERSE BACKGROUND in risk management and occupational health and safety. He served five years active duty in the U.S. Army as a Combat Engineer, achieving the rank of Sergeant. He was deployed to Baghdad, Iraq in 2004 where he served in support of Task Force 1-9 Cavalry, an element of the 1st Cavalry Division.

Brian left military service in 2005 with an honorable discharge and went to work in the open-pit copper mines of the southwestern U.S. where he first became involved in occupational health and safety. He later became the Corporate Safety Director for a multi-divisional industrial construction company.

In addition to his continued presence in the mines, Brian broadened his safety experience with operations in oil and gas, as well as pipeline industries. It was here that Brian began drafting the concept of his theory of Inversion. During a three-and-half-year stint, guided by the Inversion principles, Brian helped the company earn an OHSAS 18001 Health and Safety

Assessment Series certification, which is a globally recognized standard for safety management. This heavily contributed to reducing the company's Experience Modifier Rating (EMR) by 35 points, which greatly reduced the cost of the company's workers' compensation insurance premiums.

Brian moved on to become Environmental Health and Safety Manager for an aluminum remelt, extrusion, and fabrication operation. He continued developing the Perspective-Based Safety Culture, traveling North America to other extrusion operations to give presentations and help change the mindset of modern occupational safety.

Brian now serves as a Risk Consultant with clients in many different industries. He delivers his stories and philosophical anecdotes to help others realize the importance of perspective-based safety.

Made in United States
Orlando, FL
16 February 2022